Silent Abuse

Her Pain...My Scars

Stephanie Jefferson Martin

Silent Abuse – Her Pain, My Scars

© 2020 Stephanie Jefferson Martin

Published in the United States

ISBN: 979-8621547462

Cover Design: Shekinah Glory Publishing

Editor: Shekinah Glory Publishing

Dedication

- ❖ This book is dedicated to my mother, **Juanita Bynum Jefferson**, a woman who exemplified great strength and courage has as a very hardworking woman, who tried to understand everybody's problems. My mother possessed a great deal of love for me, although there were times, she didn't know how to show it. She encouraged me to write this book and most of all to tell my "Truth" no matter how or what people would see or think of me. Juanita was a very smart intelligent woman who evolved from earning a GED to retiring from the IRS as a Tax Examiner.

- ❖ To my father, **Clyde Jefferson Sr.**, who was always there when I needed him. He was a very humble man in all of his ways.

- ❖ To my oldest sister, **Renee Lisa Bruce** who was always willing and ready to take up for me no matter what the situation consisted of.

- ❖ To my oldest brother, **Ronald Lee Bynum Sr.**, who helped my mother raise me when I was growing up. An honorable man who fought and protected me to the end.

- ❖ To my late friend, **Sherllyn Franklin**, who was always there for me when I needed a shoulder to cry on no matter what time it was. She tried to protect me in so many ways and would be Very Proud of me for this great accomplishment.

- ❖ Last but not least to my baby son, **Terrell Martez Pitts** who showed me a great deal of love before he passed away and told me to make sure I finish this book.

Acknowledgements

- First, I want to thank God for giving me the vision in 2012 to write this book.

- My husband, **Roy Anthony Martin, Sr.**, for all of his support to help me accomplish the vision God gave me. Thank you for believing in me when I wanted to give up on writing this book. You kept telling me to trust God and if God gave me the vision, keep the Faith and Never give up. Thank you for laboring in prayer with me as a servant of God and pushing me to birth this book. His words have always been to make sure that God gets the Glory out of whatever I do.

- My Pastor, **Shockie Weathington**, for all her prayers and the faith she had in me to fulfill my dream and to take me in as her daughter.

- Pastors **John and Janice Jones**, from **Bestheda Word of Life Christian Center** in Memphis, TN. I met them during a time of my life when I didn't know which way to turn. I want to thank them both for helping me when I was at the lowest state of my life.

- ❖ My God Mother, **Marie Weeden**, who was always there when I needed a shoulder to cry on and someone that I could confide in. There were times I would call her crying, but she never said anything negative about my husband or the situation, all she would say, "Is baby let's pray!"

- ❖ My brother, **Clyde Jefferson, Jr.,** who has always had my back when I was growing up. He spoiled me throughout my entire senior year and never knew the pain I endured as a child until maybe a year ago. As a child I never witnessed my brother showing any type of emotion. When I shared my traumatic past with him, he wanted to prosecute any living violators. His exact words were, "It's Never Too Late!"

- ❖ My brother, **Stanley Eric Jefferson**, who has instilled in me that I'm a very intelligent person and I can accomplish anything that I put my mind to. Stanley has been my support throughout this entire process.

- ❖ My sister-in-law, **Mablean Bynum**, who helped my brother raise me and inspired me to keep writing this book.

- ❖ My sister, **Mentha Jefferson**, who I can always call on to listen to me vent.

- ❖ My sister, **Sherron Jefferson**, who has also been my support in the process of writing this book. After the passing of my mother she stepped into that role and kept me busy.
- ❖ My daughter, **Kenshia Boyland**, who has always been my number one cheerleader when times were tough, and I thought I couldn't make it.
- ❖ My son, **Lucious Pitts IV**, who I can never hide my pain from and if I'm sad he will talk to me to ensure that I'm ok.
- ❖ My granddaughter, **Keiarra Shantise Reed**, who has grown up to become my motivation.
- ❖ **Tory Lamont Shaw**, who has always felt my pain and wouldn't leave my side because he felt the hurt.
- ❖ **Sherry Kelly** who has been my constant support since I told her about the vision God gave me. She told me that whenever the book was finished, she's all in for whatever I needed her to help me with. **Mark Ball** for his overwhelming support. You would have thought he was writing the book because of the excitement he shared as I was telling him my vision. Sherry and Mark has always called me their little sister since I've known them.

- ❖ To my many great friends - **Cynthia Scaife, Dempsey Giden, Patricia Dorsey, Marilyn Coleman, Sherron Davis, Shelisa Jordan, Jessie Morehead, and Nancy Allen** who has been there encouraging me throughout the years of the "Silent Abuse" I sustained.

- ❖ To **James Love, Sr.,** for giving me a place to stay when I was homeless, and for believing in me when I approached him about writing my book.

- ❖ I would like to thank my three God daughters. **Tracy White** who my daughter brought home from school when she was in the seventh grade and I just fell in love with her. She would always say something to make me smile and her favorite words have always been, "God Is Somebody". **Sharon Smith** whom I met during the time my back was against the wall and she helped me get through some very difficult times. **Veronica Hunter** embraced me and loved on me in her own way because she felt the pain that I was hiding from my daughter, **Kenshia Boyland**, because I didn't want to overwhelm her with the pain that caused me to be in a depressed state of mind.

❖ I want to thank my uncle **Robert Reeves** for sharing the details he had concerning my mother's childhood. His recollection of past events was captivating. He and my mother were actually first cousins, but they were very close growing up, so I started calling him my uncle when I was a little girl because all of my mother's brothers were deceased.

❖ I would like to thank **Shekinah Glory Publishing** for helping me to birth the vision God gave me.

❖ Last but not least, **Kevin Busby**, who I met and who believed in me when I told him that I was writing this book and would periodically ask if the book had been finished.

Table of Contents

Introduction

I'm sure you've heard the classic cliché, "Silence is Golden!" Throughout my life I've learned that silence has the potential to produce great things. Silence can produce peace. Silence can interrupt disorder. Silence even causes us to hear the sweet whisper of our Savior's voice. But what happens when silence is a direct result of abuse.

Can you picture an individual yelling day in and day out, yet no matter how loud or how hard they scream, it appears that no one hears them? They are fighting to be heard, but no one hears their cries, sees their tears or notices their scars.

This individual is bleeding in plain sight, but no one seems to pay attention or simply doesn't care. This person is wounded and in need of help, but there needs go unnoticed day after day. The people around them are too consumed with self to see there is an issue.

People live their lives hurt, broken, wounded, battered, rejected, abandoned, ashamed, addicted, afflicted and dis-eased 365 days a year, 24 hours a day, 7 days a week, and have no idea how to obtain freedom. Men, women, boys and girls live life being silently abused, while mastering the ability to put bandages on their infected wounds caused by the trials and trauma of life.

They learn to hide in plain sight. Walking around smiling, laughing, talking, working, mothering, fathering, being a wife, a husband, a child – all while battling some form of emotional trauma. What puzzles me the most is how we pass these emotional traumas from generation to generation.

We fail to truly understand that our inability to heal, will continue to fester and transfer demonic strongholds from person to person – from parent to child. We were given the command by God to multiply and replenish the earth, therefore, we must understand that our demons can very well become our children's demons when we fail to recognize, repent, and allow deliverance to fully manifest in our lives.

This goes back as far as the garden. When Adam and Eve disobeyed God it brought a curse upon their lives. That same curse was thrust upon us until Jesus became the curse and died on the cross. God told Adam that man would have to work hard, and that Eve would bring forth children in painful labor. These commands are still in full effect today, but God has given us the power through Jesus Christ to overcome and be successful in working and birthing children. My point is this – what we do as parents can have a direct effect on our children. When we fail to walk in obedience to Gods word it can affect everything and everyone that is directly connected to us.

Let me be perfectly clear! I'm not sharing this because it sounds good. I'm sharing this because I lived it. My life as a child, a teenager and now a woman has been rather painful and very rough. I've treaded on some dangerous roads and found myself in places and situations that only God could deliver me from. I've encountered abuse that forced me to put a muzzle on my mouth, but this didn't start with me. This started before I was ever thought of. This cycle of silent dysfunction started with my mother – a teenage concubine.

Yes, you read that right! My mother was forced to become a teenage sex slave to a much older married man. Can you imagine what she must have experienced? What she endured? Her thoughts and fears day after day? Her mental capacity to even understand what was happening to her. The pain of losing her innocence against her will!

Well, unfortunately she wouldn't be the only one. I, being one of her daughters had to travel down some of her same roads. Her PAIN - BECAME MY SCARS! The enemy tried to destroy my life as well, but God had another plan. There was a ransom for my life, but the Glory of God stepped in and declared it PAID IN FULL! You see that is what I desire to put on display in this book. Yes, this book is about my testimony and to share some of the hardships I've encountered, but more than anything it is to glorify God for keeping me when I couldn't keep myself.

The enemy tried to drown out God's glorious light with his darkness, but God equipped me with the power to overcome. The enemy wanted me to focus on the negative things, but God wanted me to focus on His glory! Those before me may have missed the mark and chosen to remain in dark places, but He was calling me out of my pit of darkness, up to the mountain to dwell in His cloud of glory.

Can you imagine how empowered Moses must have felt when he came down off the mountain after being in the midst of Gods glory for forty days and forty nights? The word says his face was glowing so much he had to wear a veil.

My God! It didn't have anything to do with where he came from or the mistakes he made along the way. It was all about obedience and his willingness to follow God and obey. I believe Moses realized that his past life couldn't define him any longer because in the presence of God is fullness of joy.

Today, I decree and declare that we are full of Gods joy and by the end of this book you will be basking in His glory. By the end of this book you will know the power of repentance and breaking generational curses. You will have a strong desire to see yourself, your spouse, your children, family members, co-workers, community and nation healed, delivered and set FREE! For the word says, "Whom the Son sets FREE, is FREE indeed!"

Chapter One

A Broken Family Foundation

Train up a child in the way he should go; even when he is old, he will not depart from it. Proverbs 22:6

God ordained family from the very beginning of creation. The intent was for us to live free and happy in the earth, with God providing our every need while we worship and live in harmony with Him. There was never supposed to be any pain, trials, and hardships. After the fall of Adam and Eve, Cain killed Abel, and this started a domino effect of broken family foundations. To the point where later down the line one of Cain's distant relatives killed a man and said, "If Cain was vindicated 7 times, I will be vindicated 77 times." The sinful nature of man became so bad in the earth, that God destroyed it and said, "It grieved His heart that He ever made man."

Spirits can enter a family bloodline and wreak havoc when left unresolved. John 10:10 says, "The enemy comes to kill, steal, and to destroy." His job is to destroy the family bloodline and to ensure that abundant blessings are not rendered by God. The issues in my family began long before both me and my mother were created. We have no clue how far back the demonic strongholds of perversion and rejection go in our bloodline, but I'm determined through the power of God to put a stop to its deadly forces.

This brings me to May 19, 2016. This was one of the hardest days of my life. This was the day I lost my mother. I thought I was prepared because God had already forewarned me that she would transition at 7:00pm on that day. I arrived at the hospital and walked into the room at 6:55pm. My brother and his wife, along with the pastor and his wife were already in the room.

The Lord spoke to me and said she was getting ready to transition, so we began singing and praising God. Once I realized that she was actually gone, I went into a state of shock. I felt like something on the inside of me was uprooted and snatched out of my life. I had never experienced a feeling quite like this before. The tears were streaming down my face, and these weren't tears of sadness, because I was happy that she wasn't suffering anymore, and that she was now absent from the body, but present with the Lord.

My mother started going blind in 1993. She encountered not one, but two heart bypass surgeries. She was diabetic and when she went to the hospital before her passing, they diagnosed her with a rare blood disease. From this she never came back home. I've heard people say, "Sometimes people have to die, for others to live." I'm not sure if I believed this or not, but today I'm a living proof that there is some truth to this statement.

After my mother passed, I felt like a new person. I felt like a prisoner who had been shackled to her my entire life. It felt as if her pain was my pain and her anger over time became my anger. No matter what I tried to do in life, it appeared that I couldn't escape the shadow of the very demons that taunted her during her life. It wasn't until her death that I began to sense a bit of freedom in my life. I started to feel like I could breath. I spent so much time feeling as if I had a target on my back and that I was destined to meet destruction instead of my destiny.

If I could describe it in one word, it would be "rebirth". Even though God was doing a new thing in my life, I didn't want to believe that she was gone. I grieved for quite some time, but eventually God showed up and gave me peace about her new dwelling place. During my mother's life on earth, she experienced a great deal of torment and dysfunction.

Her father's father, my great-grandfather was from Mound Bayou, Mississippi. This city is notable for having been founded as an independent black community in 1887 by former slaves led by Isaiah Montgomery. There are twelve pioneers from Davis Bend that still exist today. My great grandfather supposedly killed a white man during that time, and no one knows whether he was killed or disappeared to start a new life.

This caused my great-grandmother to pack up and move to Memphis. My mother's father grew up in Memphis, met a woman who was half white and they had two children, a boy and a girl. That girl was my grandmother, my mother's mama. Unfortunately, she died when my mother was only twelve years old, so I never got a chance to meet her. This was devastating for my mother. Not just the passing of her mother, but the fact that she had to be moved around from family member to family member.

She finally settled in with her aunt, her mother's sister. One would think that this would have been a good thing. Who would take better care of my mother than the one person who knew her mother best? They were sisters and this was her niece. Well, this may be the case in most situations, but it turned out to be something entirely different. My mother's aunt was a Madame. Yes, she was like Dolly Pardon, running, "The Best Little Whorehouse" in Memphis.

Again, my mother was only twelve years old when she moved in. There was one particular patron who noticed and took a liking to my twelve year old mother. This man was triple her age, plus he was married with children. My aunt told the gentlemen that my mother would be more tender at the age of fourteen, so he waited.

Can you imagine this man waiting two years just to sleep with a child? How sick, twisted and perverted can you be? When my mother turned fourteen, her aunt couldn't wait to make a profit off of her. How do you sell your own flesh and blood? She sold my mother to this man like they were back during the times of slavery.

My mother became this man's personal property. He rented an apartment for my mother to live in by herself. He would come and sleep with her and then go home to his wife on the other side of town. This was beyond sickening and even unbelievable, but it was true. My mother became this man's concubine and she had to do whatever pleased him. A "concubine" is a woman who lives with a man but has lower status than his wife. She was an innocent teenage girl, with no mother and father, and no authentic support from her family. I have often tried to mentally place myself in her shoes during that time, and no matter what it seems so unreal.

I can only imagine how she felt, what she thought, how much she cried and maybe wanted to die. I'm almost certain those would have been my reactions. It wasn't long before my mother became pregnant with her first child. Fifteen and pregnant by a man old enough to be her father. Instead of being a typical teenage girl, experiencing her first kiss and getting ready for high school; she was cooped up in an apartment learning how to become a woman to a predator.

She didn't have anyone there to guide her or teach her about life. She had to learn about the birds and the bees through painful experience. Her entire childhood snatched away from her at the hands of two spiritually perverse individuals. How can anyone sleep or live with themselves after doing such a thing? How can a man even bring himself to sleep with a child? These are the questions I pondered over and over again, once I learned the details of my mothers' story.

Situations like these make you ask the question, "Why God?", but then His word will say, "His grace is sufficient and that ALL things work together for the good of those who love God and who are called according to His purpose." All of this was going on and no one knew about it. My mother was forced to remain "silent" about the trauma she was experiencing.

How could anything good come out of such a horrible situation? How could any light shine forth from this pit of darkness? Unfortunately, that was for God to determine and not man.

He had my mothers' path already planned before she was conceived in her mother's womb. At some point my teenage mother started going to church. Some of the older seasoned women in the church noticed that she was a young girl trying to raise a son all alone and needed help. They took her under their wings and taught her how to be a young woman and a mother.

This was a blessing in disguise, but needless to say she was still confused about life and hurt. She was traumatized at the fact that this man treated her like less than a human being. It was all about him, but what about her feelings and emotions. What about the mental anguish she would have to endure throughout the span of her life? It amazes me how people fail to think of the long term effects of their actions when they are trying to fulfill temporary gratifications.

When an individual is violated, the violator is only thinking about that moment, but the violated has to live with the pain, scars and memories for a lifetime. No matter how much my mother loved God, I know she battled internally. It was evident in her life and how she raised me and my other siblings.

At some point my mother became frustrated and tried to escape her owner at the age of seventeen by getting married to another man. She jumped out of the pot, and into the frying pan, by leaving one bad situation for another. I'm sure its safe to assume that anything was better than being someone's sex slave. Well, during the union she birth two more daughters and another son. In her early twenties she had a total of four children and was still unhappy and unsettled.

The ungodly soul tie that was created with the man who bought her and made her his concubine, had not been broken. Eventually she left her husband and went back to the man who owned her. It wasn't long before she became pregnant again and together, they had another child, a daughter. You would think this cycle of dysfunction would have stopped there, but it didn't.

She became weary with her owner and went back to the husband, became pregnant and had another son. This was a total of 6 children between the husband and the man who sexually abused her. Some would think this was absolutely absurd or that I was making this story up, but this was my mother's life that she was living day in and day out. Honestly, I don't know how she did it? How she juggled the painful emotions? I just don't think I could have done it, but God said He wouldn't put more on us than we could bear, so He knew just how much she could take.

People, emotional bondage is real! Strongholds are real. Soul ties are real. Unhealthy dysfunctional relationships are like cancers, that eat away at your self-esteem, dignity, and self-worth until you are spiritually and sometimes physically dead. I believe that my mother was spiritually dead, and she was trying to find life and light by any means necessary.

But that wasn't the end of my mother's journey, because then came me. It was unclear who my father was, but before she passed it was confirmed that my father was supposedly a preacher who passed away years ago. As you can see the foundation of my mother's existence was very broken and distorted. Here you have this woman with seven children who was sexually violated and forced to live a life of displeasure. She adopted a survival mentality that caused her to do just enough to live each day. I mean can you blame her.

Honestly, I did! I blamed her for her inability to truly open up and love me for me, but today as I journey back over my own life, that was impossible. She couldn't give, what she never received. As children we don't understand this concept, until we get grown and start having our own kids. My mother did the best she could with what she had.

I wouldn't be the woman I am today, had she not been strong enough to press pass her inner demons and daily struggles. I have to admit; that perversion demon that embedded itself in my mother's womb, wasn't only sent to destroy her, but everything attached to her. Even though she was no longer dealing with the man who stole her innocence, he engraved himself in her soul through the anger and bitterness she carried towards him.

It wouldn't be long before that spirit of perversion would present itself in my life and attack at will. The enemy knew he couldn't come the same way, but he found other ways to disguise himself in my life. I only wish that my mother had been strong enough to recognize the signs of sexual abuse that I was encountering.

Chapter Two

Broken Innocence

The Lord is my light and my salvation; whom shall I fear? the Lord is the strength of my life; of whom shall I be afraid? When the wicked, even mine enemies and my foes, came upon me to eat up my flesh, they stumbled and fell. Psalms 27:1-2

Innocence is priceless! There is no value that can be placed on the innocence of a child. How sweet it is to be a child that is free to simply be a child without disruption or destruction. The joys of playing with dolls and trains. The pure laughter of a child is soothing and pleasant. They are worry free, having no fears and willing to take risk without fail. One would think that the enemy wouldn't go after an innocent child, but that is when he does the most damage.

This is when he wreaks the most havoc, because a child doesn't know anything about spiritual warfare and has no clue how to recognize or rebuke the enemy. To be honest many parents don't have the spiritual discernment to see when the enemy is attacking their child or children. Therefore, the enemy steps in and strategizes to destroy the purpose and plan before we even come into the full understanding of who God created us to be.

I had to learn this the hard way. You would think that after what my mother experienced, she would have been on alert at all times when it came to the enemy and his sneak attacks, but that wasn't the case. She was battling her own demons, plus trying to provide for seven children. I started being bullied in the first grade and it lasted all the way to sixth grade. The enemy didn't waste anytime coming for me. He had people on assignment waiting to attack at all times.

I would ask my teacher if I could leave early because these two brothers always tried to beat me up after school. Before school they took my lunch money and after school, they waited to jump me almost every day. My brother's house was my safe haven even when he told me I couldn't come over for the weekend because he had something to do. I didn't care, I would hide in the back of his car and wouldn't get up until they got home to find out I was hiding in the back seat.

I didn't know how to explain that I was being bullied. To this day, I don't know why I didn't just tell my big brother. I was being silently abused and didn't even realize it. I became introverted and isolated. I didn't want to be around anyone. I was feeling some type of way and I didn't like the feeling. I was angry and afraid. All I wanted to do was run away all the time. I didn't know how to stand up to the bullies and express that they were causing me pain. I just surrendered to the abuse and didn't even try to fight. I thought about running away from home so many times it was unreal, but I didn't have anywhere to go. The crazy thing is that I didn't know I was being abused.

When I was around five years old, my mother moved me and my siblings to a new town. When I was seven years old, there was this fifteen year old boy who started hanging around me. As a little kid, I just saw him as an older kid who was just bigger than me, but he had other things on his mind. One day he got me in a place where he could touch me. He put his hands in my underwear and started fondling me.

I didn't really understand what he was doing, but I knew it wasn't right. I didn't like it. I didn't feel right. When he finished, he told me that I better not tell anyone. Again, there I was being abused out in the open, but forced to remain silent, which was the instruction of the abuser. I followed his instruction and didn't say anything.

From the time I was born my oldest brother helped to take care of me. He had his own place, so I would go to his house on the weekends. I couldn't wait because it was my escape from being molested by the boy.

Over a period of time I became very isolated and withdrawn. I can't recall my mother or anyone teaching me about sex or what to do if someone touches you against your will. I was never taught that no one, especially a male should touch you in inappropriate places. I wasn't taught not to talk to strangers. So, I went with the flow, because I didn't know any better.

When I was ten years old, I played with this little girl who was the same age. She and I would visit the nursing home to see the "candy man" which was an old man who sold candy. Not thinking anything of it, other than the desire to fulfill our sugar cravings. Well this man had a few cravings of his own and that was to take advantage of two innocent little girls.

This man fondled both of us on several occasions. Again, two naïve little girls who wanted candy and fell prey to another attack of the enemy. He was trying to embed fear and emotional trauma by any means necessary. He didn't care who he used. At the time my mother couldn't afford a place that was big enough for everyone. I made myself comfortable in the closet because I didn't want to share a bed or room with my sister. I put a nightstand in the closet and blankets on the floor to make a pallet and the closet became my own personal safe haven. Every time I was violated, or something happened, I went straight to the closet.

Right before I turned 14, I met this guy that I really liked, and I thought he liked me. One day my mother went to church and I didn't go, but she instructed me to stay in the house. Well, I was being hardheaded and went outside and snuck around the corner to meet the boy. He took me to his house and led me up the stairs into a room. Oddly, he left out the room and closed the door. I sat there waiting on him, when this grown man opens the door and walks in.

I wasn't sure if this was a joke or not, but apparently the joke was on me. He insisted that I take my clothes off and not try to fight. Considering the fact, I had been in this situation several times before, I knew the deal and the drill. I tried to fight, but he was too strong. Once my clothes were off, he performed oral sex on me which was disgusting. Then he tried to force himself into me while I laid there listless and afraid. I started screaming to the top of my lungs, then he stopped. The enemy was very angry because he was not successful in his dirty act. I just knew the boy I called myself liking was coming in to take part in this hideous act, but instead since his uncle couldn't finish violating me, they told me to get out.

I was so lost and ashamed. I trusted this person and again I was violated. It was starting to feel like I had a stamp on my forehead that read, "I want to be sexually violated!" I couldn't tell my mother what happened because I wasn't supposed to be out of the house. I had to bite the bullet on this one.

Then I met this guy at the Community Center, who seemed to be very quiet, so I fell for his cleverness. I was looking for attention in all the wrong places and believe me, I was about to get what I was looking for. After practice he would walk me home and say nice things to me.

I finally met someone who actually liked me for a chance, so I thought. Once again, I failed to realize that the enemy was setting up another demonic tactic to get what he wanted. I was young and didn't fully understand the concept of relationships. Up to this point I hadn't witnessed a healthy relationship. Although, I had been sexually violated, I was still a virgin. We started dating and he forced me to have sex with him. Not long after I found out I was pregnant. I lost my virginity and gained a baby. The generational cycle continued. I was pregnant at the tender age of fourteen, just like my mother.

When I realized I was pregnant I told my oldest sister. She suggested an abortion, but when our mother found out she said she would have my sister arrested. We actually went to the abortion clinic and started the process, but when my sister found out that my mom was going to have her arrested, we stopped the procedures. The curse continued. When my mother found out she was very angry but didn't want me to abort the baby. We exchanged some choice words that led to her slapping me.

I was torn! I knew it wasn't right for me to be pregnant at fourteen. I knew this would put an extra strain on her, because not only was I pregnant, but all three of my sisters were teenage moms. Matter of fact my oldest sister had two babies. This was the part that puzzled me. I was the baby of the family, which meant someone should have schooled me on sex and boys, but that wasn't the case. We were living her life, and since she was forced to suffer in silence, we were all following in her footsteps. No one was allowed to share their struggles. The word says, "My people suffer for a lack of knowledge." Well, I will be the first to admit that we were suffering because no one was willing to teach the other based on their mistakes.

At this point I pretty much felt like my life was over. I was a baby having a baby while harboring secrets of sexual abuse. I often wondered had my mother known I was being abused; if she would have been still been angry or embraced me knowing that her baby was repeating the traumatic encounters of her life. Unfortunately, I will never know the answer because I didn't say anything. I suffered in silence. I suffered with the muffled thoughts of abuse I sustained and now I was pregnant. I wasn't prepared for my childhood to be over. I didn't know how to take care of a child. I was a child myself.

The misery of being pregnant became more overwhelming than being molested. Being a mother was a lifelong commitment and even though my mother provided for us, I didn't really know what it felt like to be nurtured. My mother was not an affectionate person.

She focused on working and taking care of her children. After divorcing her husband, she never allowed another man to live with us again.

At the time my brother was in the military. I wrote him a letter to vent about the tension between me and mama. Well, my nosy sister read the letter and told me to contact DHS, but then turned around and told my mother about the letter. I felt like a stepchild. There were times I didn't eat, and I had to sleep on the floor pregnant.

Before I got pregnant my mother spoiled me, but afterwards, she became bitter towards me. In my heart I believe she was disappointed. I was the last girl and I'm sure she wanted something different for me. My sisters were living her life and I was the only hope left.

I understand if these were her feelings, but not one time did she consider that something could have led me down this road or that it may have been destined. God is the Creator of life and He determines when someone is born and who they are born to.

Listening to my sister, I contacted DHS. They came and took me away from the home and placed me in an all-girls home for girls who were being abused. There are no words to describe how I felt. Life wasn't good at home, but it was better than being around a bunch of people I didn't know. I was pregnant without a permanent resident for me and my unborn child. When I gave birth to my daughter, I didn't know what to expect. I was terribly frightened, but I was by myself.

I knew my mother was angry, but she knew how it felt to birth at children at fifteen with no help, no support, no guidance, and no love. She was blessed with the seasoned saints who stepped in and helped her, but she couldn't put her differences aside to do the same thing for her own child.

Despite the issues with my mom, I couldn't turn back the hands of time. I couldn't change the fact that I was a teenage mother and I definitely couldn't change what happened in her life. As much as I wanted to, I couldn't stop in the middle of the race. I arrived at a place where I wanted to throw in the towel, but there was a still small voice that kept pushing me along.

God gave me the strength to birth my daughter. Even though I'd been beaten down and broken, I was proud to be her mother. When I looked into her eyes, I knew that God blessed me despite of me, which meant I had to do right by her. I refused to make the same mistakes I experienced at the hands of my mother. I wouldn't wish that feeling on my worst enemy.

After having my baby, we went to live with my brother and his wife. My mother didn't want me and her granddaughter in her home. This was devastating, but there was nothing I could do about it. I had to deal with the cards dealt to me and it wasn't a pretty hand at all.

It's one thing to be homeless by yourself but being homeless with a child, while being a child is mentally exhausting. There were times I wanted to give the baby away and end my life, but I had to keep pressing. The enemy wanted me to throw up the white flag, but I wasn't ready to surrender. It was hard, but I was willing to see it through to the end, even though I had no clue what the end looked like.

I was walking in faith and didn't even know what it was. God had His hand in my life and when I wanted to turn to the left or the right, a force unbeknownst to myself would push me forward. I had to make each day count to the best of my ability. I had to drop my pride and move in with the mother of my child's father. I didn't want to intrude on her because she had her own family to care for, but the love she had in her heart for God caused her to embrace me and my daughter.

Now her trifling son on the other hand, was something altogether different. Nevertheless, he even tried to get this other boy to have sex with me so he could put the baby on him. I started getting welfare for me and the baby. Every month, like clockwork, her father would jump on me and take the check. He took other girls out, while I sat at home with our baby. He never took me and the baby anywhere. It felt like he was ashamed of us.

Oftentimes, I thought I wasn't pretty enough for him because he never spent time with me. The only time he acknowledged me was at the first of the month or if he wanted to have sex. His mother and father helped me all the time, but he did nothing. He started becoming physically and verbally abusive. He slapped me around and this caused me to become fearful of him. Like every other violation, I accepted it in silence.

I didn't have the courage to tell anyone I was being silently abused by the father of my child and it didn't feel good. For the first two years of my daughter's life I wanted to commit suicide because I felt unwanted and unloved. I found myself crying all the time because I couldn't understand what was happening to my life. I was only a young teenage mother trying to do the best I could for my child. But no matter which way I turned disaster was staring me in the face. I felt like I was stuck with this abusive man who didn't love me or his child.

Again, I kept feeling something tugging at me to keep pressing. God was forcing me to keep going. When I felt like I had no hope, He would show up and remind me just how strong I really was. Even though I was experiencing a wealth of trauma I managed to keep a 3.8 grade point average in high school. I became a member of the National Honor Society, graduating at only sixteen years old. This was nothing but the favor and grace of God!

During my senior year I looked forward to prom, but I wasn't able to participate. My daughter's father attended several proms, but never asked me to attend one of them or even took into consideration that I wanted to attend my own.

When my daughter turned four years old, I was finally able to detach myself from him. Let me be clear, I didn't make this decision on my own, he pretty much made it for me. One day he flipped out and jumped on me until my eye was black and blue. This time my oldest brother got involved. The days of silent abuse came to a temporary end. My brother tracked him down and beat his butt. He never laid a hand on me again. I was finally free of his abuse and could exhale.

Despite the four years of hell, I pushed through and God kept me. There were days I didn't think I would make it to graduation. I didn't think I would be in the right mental space to take care of my daughter. But God!!

I didn't fully understand God or how He worked, but I knew that He had to be doing something in my life for me to get up and have the strength to fight another day. As I continued my journey, I didn't know what was next for me and my daughter. I was hoping for good things to manifest, but the enemy had someone else on assignment waiting and lurking to make their move.

Chapter Three

A Decade of Living Hell

Attend unto my cry; for I am brought very low: deliver me from my persecutors; for they are stronger than I. Bring my soul out of prison, that I may praise thy name: the righteous shall compass me about; for thou shalt deal bountifully with me. Psalms 142:6-7

A decade sounds like a very long time, but in all actuality, it is only the time span of ten years, which is approximately 3,650 days. This may seem ordinary to some, but for me there was nothing ordinary about suffering day in and day out for nearly 3000 days of my life. I'm not going to say I didn't have some good days, which is why I said 3000, but there were more bad days, than there were good days.

After graduation I was focused on taking care of my baby and making every attempt to start my life after high school. Technically, even though I graduated early I knew I wasn't going to be allowed to sit around and do nothing. I had to create a plan and quick. One day I was visiting with one of my classmates and her brother came home from the military on leave. I was sitting there minding my business when he approached me, and we started talking.

I can't say that I was looking for a relationship, but before I knew it, we were talking all the time. He was such a smooth talker. He knew just what to say to make me feel wanted and special. Something that I hadn't experienced up to that point.

In the beginning he did everything for me. At the time I felt like being his woman was a part of my new plan. After growing up in such an unstable environment I was simply longing for stability. He was in the military so having a place to live and finances wouldn't be a problem. At the time I felt like anything was better than me and my baby going from pillar to post. After dating a year, he asked me to marry him. I was only seventeen, which meant we had to get parental consent to get married.

My father, the one listed on my birth certificate, signed and gave his consent. My mother on the other hand, said she didn't want to have anything to do with me getting married. We were married in 1983. I can't begin to say how excited I was to begin this new life as a wife, living on the military base. Well only time would tell that I didn't quite know my new husband as well as I thought. He was talking one way and living another.

He was showing me the good side of him as long as I was his girlfriend, but when I became his wife, he changed. After we settled in together, the cat jumped out the bag. I married an alcoholic. Being that I was only seventeen, I didn't really know what that entailed, but it didn't take very long for me to find out. It didn't take long for the alcohol to take control of the relationship. He started to become very mean and abusive.

The first time he abused me, he left his handprint on my face, because he slapped me just that hard. I really thought I had escaped this life of abuse. I just knew he was different and that me and my daughter would have a better life. My time to breathe was short lived because the more he drank, the more he beat me.

He would call me names and treat me like I was nobody. This wasn't what I pictured for my life. This was supposed to be my ticket away from abuse, not a ticket into more abuse. No matter how bad it got, he would always come back after he sobered up and beg for forgiveness. Being young wasn't really working in my favor, because he was treating me more like a daughter than a woman.

I didn't know how to handle the situation, so no matter what, I stayed. I know this sounds stupid, but I was exhausted. I didn't have any fight left in me, so I did my best to stay out of his way. I worked overtime to avoid making him angry when I knew he had been drinking. It was evident that he had a lot of emotional issues he was dealing with and I just happened to be the closest person to take them out on.

I struggled with loving him. There were times that I hated him. Times I wanted to kill him and sometimes myself. It was just too much. The crazy thing is, he knew he was doing wrong by me and my daughter. He would beat me and then turn around and hide our clothes so we couldn't leave.

What I thought was going to be a lovely marriage, turned out to be a living hell. After being married a couple of years, he was going to be stationed in Germany, which meant as his wife, I had to go as well. We were in Germany from 1985 to 1990.

Can you imagine being in a foreign place, with no family and friends for five years? I was still being abused, but his wrath escalated from physical abuse to infidelity. He was so bold; he would actually bring other women into our home, while I was at work. My five year old daughter would tell me that other women were in the house. He didn't even have enough decency to hide the women from my daughter.

In 1986, I got pregnant with our first child and delivered a bouncing baby boy. Then to top it off, it was rumored that another girl was pregnant with his child at the same time I was. Quite naturally he denied it.

What should have been a joyful experience for me, turned out to be overwhelming and painful. It got so bad that I contemplated suicide. I took a bottle of pills with the intent of taking my life, but it didn't work. I was so upset, because I didn't see any other options. I felt like I was in prison. My heart, mind, soul, and spirit were all being vexed and trampled on at the same time. I was still, but I didn't even feel like a woman. I mean to be honest I didn't even feel like a human.

I had finally reached the point of no return and I needed help and I mean quick. I grew up in the church, therefore, I knew about God, but I didn't know God. One day I was led to visit this church. While I was there, I wasn't experiencing the tormenting thoughts and feelings of rage. I felt an overwhelming sense of peace.

The church became a safe haven for me. It reminded me of my brothers back seat when I was being bullied and my closet at my mother's house after being molested.

Eventually, I started going to church all the time, to avoid going home. I was singing in the choir and serving faithfully in the church. Through all this I couldn't understand why I was still being beat. I was being persecuted for righteousness sake and I had to realize that he was battling his own demons that he couldn't control.

God was doing something new in my life that I couldn't quite comprehend or explain. I was experiencing an internal peace, even though I was living in an external hell. In my new quest I began to see myself through a different set of lenses. The lies I'd been forced to believe about myself based on the actions of others wasn't true. God created me in His image and His likeness, and I didn't have to take the abuse anymore. I didn't have to be afraid anymore, because God was helping me to understand that He would provide for me. I didn't have to settle, as long as I was willing to trust in the Lord with all my heart.

One day I woke up and realized that he wasn't going to change. I had to do something different for me and my children. I thought that giving him a son would calm him down, but life for us only grew worse, especially when I started going to church. It was like he hated me and no matter how hard I tried I couldn't please him.

Even after he would beat me, he still demanded sex and though it would make me sick to my stomach I still honored my vows as his wife. I would still cook, clean, shine his boots and make sure that his uniform was ready for work. I can never explain how I was able to do this but believe me it wasn't in my own strength.

One day he beat me so bad that I didn't think I was going to live. He begged me not to go to his First Sergeant, but I needed a plan and I needed one quick, or I wasn't going to be alive. At some point, the enemy opened the door to my heart and walked right on in. I started feeling anger and rage towards him that was probably uncommon to man. I wanted blood! I wanted him dead!

I started thinking about all the beatings, how my face was constantly black and blue, the pain, the hurt, the shame of being treated worse than an animal, the cheating and the name calling. I was hearing voices prompting me to kill him.

I envisioned myself grabbing a hammer, during one of his drunken stupors and beating him in the head until there was no more breath in his body. I could feel myself hitting him. I was losing my mind and I didn't know what to do. All of a sudden, I snapped, and I was led to call this lady at church, which was my god-mother. I told her everything I was feeling, and she instructed me to catch a cab to her house so she could pray for me.

The hand of God was upon my life, because at that moment I chose good over evil. I chose to allow God to vindicate me, instead of me vindicating myself and ending up in a real prison. God's grace was truly sufficient that night.

I was temporarily mentally insane, and God delivered me with His saving grace once I opened my heart to repent of my evil thoughts. He gave me a peace that surpassed my minute understanding. I am very proud to say that God saved and delivered me for real at that moment. I never felt the presence of God like that before. God delivered my mind so I could continue to live for Him and see His glory.

After this, I mustered up the courage to talk to his First Sergeant about the abuse and I requested that he send me home.

I had no clue how this was going to work. I was afraid that he wouldn't understand. I wasn't sure if he was going to tell my husband and that would cause him to become even more angry and that the beatings would probably be worse than the others. There were so many negative thoughts rumbling through my head and then I decided to simply trust that God would make a way.

Well, the First Sergeant granted my request and sent me and my two children back home. I was so excited and happy. I had no clue what awaited us when we arrived, but I didn't have to worry about being beat and mistreated anymore. My husband on the other hand divorced me in 1992 and married someone else. Good ridding's!

I just knew I was home free and going to get a break from trauma after leaving him. He was gone, but now I had to deal with something that spilled over from our marriage. My daughter loved my now ex-husband very much. I am grateful that he never mistreated my daughter. He treated her like she was his own child.

That was the man she knew as her father, but as a child she didn't understand the pressure I was under and the abuse that I was enduring. All she saw was that I snatched her away from the one man she loved, respected, and who provided for her. This caused my baby to fall into a deep depression. She was only twelve years old. The same age my mother was when she lost her mother. These demonic strongholds were truly making there rounds through each generation with the assignment to mentally destroy us.

This spirit of mental oppression was so strong over my daughter that I had to put her in a facility called Lakeside. That was the hardest thing I think I ever had to do. I prayed night and day for God to heal my baby. I carried some guilt for a little while because she was fine, before the divorce. I finally realized that I did the right thing and God gave me peace. God healed my baby and she came home from the facility.

Just when I thought again that I was going to get a break, the enemy reared his ugly head once again. My daughter got pregnant at the age of thirteen. I was infuriated, with this generational cycle that didn't want to break. First my mother, then me, and now my daughter. I was very hurt and disappointed because guilt tried to consume me and convince me that I wasn't being a good mother. When we returned back to the states, I didn't really have any help, because my family didn't deal with us.

For some reason, they assumed that I thought I was better than them. I was far from better, I was struggling in every way possible, but it wasn't worth going through the trouble of trying to prove that. The only one I was obligated to prove anything to was ME. God was helping me to understand this more and more each day. So, I decided that I needed to further my education, in hopes that this would provide a better lifestyle for me, my children, and the grandchild who was on the way.

I started attending Memphis State University. There were times I had to leave them home alone, because I was trying to work and go to school. I was determined to break the cycles of dysfunction that I lived through in my own life.

I was trying to juggle a lot by myself, which means dating shouldn't have been in the equation AT ALL! Well, some kind of way I made time. Today, I realize I was trying to fill a fleshly void that stemmed from rejection and abandonment. In my heart I knew that God was enough, but in my flesh, I needed to be needed. I met this guy through my nephew, and we were just hanging out and having sex. What was supposed to be casual sex, eventually turned into pregnancy number three.

I can't begin to tell you the thoughts that were running through my mind. Now I was a mother of two and a grandma, with another baby on the way. I wasn't even in a committed relationship with this man. Actually, I lost contact with him, around three months into the pregnancy. When I told him, I was pregnant, he denied that the baby was his and told me to get an abortion.

I was still having a cycle with the pregnancy, so I must admit I considered taking his advice. My mother and sister convinced me not to, so I made the choice to keep the baby. Four months later I went into premature labor and had to be rushed to the hospital.

There was a unique irony about that day. I was being rushed to the hospital with no clue as to what was going on with my baby. At the same time the father of my baby had been shot and killed on his front porch. As I was entering the hospital to deliver his baby, his body was laying cold and lifeless in the same hospital. Ironically, I saw the incident on the news, but didn't realize that it was my son's father until months later. One night I was feeling rather strange. I was only eight months pregnant and my son wanted to come out that very night. But God said not so.

Well a month later, I went into labor and my mother rushed me to the hospital. I developed toxemia which caused my blood pressure to shoot up to the 300's. The doctors didn't know if neither one of us was going to make it, but God knew it wasn't our time.

I delivered a handsome baby boy. Although I was mentally drained, I was a bit excited. I just wanted his dad to see him, even if he didn't want to have anything to do with him. Well unfortunately, that wasn't going to happen.

I called his house and his mom told me that he was deceased. Oh boy was I thrown for a loop. When she gave me all the details of where, how, and when I went into a state of disbelief. I had to grasp for air because I had a panic attack. I couldn't believe what I was hearing.

Him getting killed wasn't really a shock to me because someone was trying to kill him while we were dating. His car was shot up one time while he was at my house. I looked him in the eyes, and they were orange, and the Lord revealed to me that death was upon him.

I was in shock that I had to raise another baby by myself. During this time my oldest son was very unhappy. I chalked it up to them not having a solid father figure. Therefore, I tried to overcompensate through material things. Now when I think back, I'm sure they would have wanted me, but I was working and trying to finish school.

It was to create a better life for us all, but as children they didn't see that. All they saw was that I was making matters worse, by being gone and then having more babies, which took time away from them. I was only twenty-eight years old and that decade of my life was pure hell. I kept thinking I was making the right moves, but somehow life kept getting twisted up and turned around.

I would date other men, but nothing was ever long term. I mean was it me? Was it the men I was choosing? At the time I couldn't distinguish between the two. I had been victimized so much, pointing the finger at everyone else always made the most sense, but was it true. Were there things about me, that I needed to deal with? Was I not facing the cold hard facts about me?

I needed to work on Stephanie. I hadn't had an opportunity to breathe. I was dealing with men and popping out babies. I didn't know who I was or what I wanted. I was forced to provide by any means necessary, which meant long days and even longer hours. There was little to no time for me. As much as I hated the way I was raised as a child, I was doing the same exact thing my mother did. I was living her life all over again!

Chapter Four

Living While Dead

But because of his great love for us, God, who is rich in mercy, made us alive with Christ even when we were dead in transgressions—it is by grace you have been saved. Ephesians 2:4-5

Have you ever heard of the movie, "The Walking Dead"? This may seem a little drastic, but this is how I started to feel. I felt like I wasn't living. I was just existing. My life had become routine. I was living without meaning and this wasn't the will of God for my life. I had allowed my past, my parents, my children, my downfalls, and basically all the negative things in my life to define me. Each day I was going with the flow.

When I look back, I realize that it was a learned behavior. Even though I was aspiring to do better and be better than my mother, I was still mirroring many things from her life. I guess that's why we should never say never or why the bible tells us not to judge, because we actually fall in the same ditches as the people we judge.

Life is funny like that! We go about each day having a desire for something different, which sets us on a journey of searching. For me, I had been looking for love in all the wrong places. I should have been starting on the inside with me, but I did the opposite and looked for love from others. Well, these people couldn't treat me any better than I treated myself and to be honest I didn't know how to treat me. All I knew was abuse and the lack of love.

My mother never taught me how a woman should be treated. She taught me how to survive and to have babies, because that is what I saw growing up. Then she treated me so cold sometimes, therefore, I didn't have that nurturing love of a mother, or the embrace of a father.

I was literally doing the best I could, with what I had to work with and that wasn't a lot. As always, I wrestled with these dysfunctions while trying to convince myself and others that I was going to focus on me. You know how we do! We have those deep conversations where we try to convince ourselves and others that enough is enough and that change starts NOW!

I had those conversations all the time. They sounded good, but when it came time to put some action behind those words, I folded every time. Like I stated previously I was dating guys here and there, but nothing serious until 2000. I met this guy from the neighborhood who I went to school with but never dated.

We started dating not long after running back into one another. As always everything started out great. We were going out and having fun, but somehow, he ended up moving in with me. This should have been a red flag, but I ignored it. After he moved in, his true character manifested, and we started fighting all the time. I couldn't believe I was going through drama all over again. I was too busy to really focus on the fighting. I set my focus on helping him get situated and active so he could leave me alone. I helped him to find a job, thinking that it would make things better.

After living together for some time, I gave him an ultimatum. He either had to move out or get married, because I didn't believe in shacking. What was I thinking? That's right I wasn't thinking. I was so busy focusing on trying to be right before God, that I missed the big picture. God was and should have been enough. I was in my own place, which meant I didn't necessarily need him, and it should have been the door hitting him where the good Lord split him, but in my brokenness I was afraid to stand up for me. I was afraid to take a stand for myself. I was still trying to appease him at my expense. In 2002, despite all the red flags we got married. Yes, I did it again! Again, I wasn't thinking clearly, I was making moves based on fear and emotions. As you can see that's a bad combination.

Somehow, I thought it was going to make a difference and lighten some of the load I had been carrying on my own for years. Let me say that wasn't the case. After I helped him get a job, he met a lady at work and started cheating with her. Yes, this ungrateful man took everything I was doing for granted and started seeing another woman, while married and living in my house.

He was a narcissist. He became verbally, physically, and mentally abusive towards me, but he chose to marry me because he didn't want to lose his security blanket. He never wanted to marry me, but he grew accustomed to what I could provide. I think this was the lowest I had felt in life, because in the other abusive marriage I was depending on him. This time I didn't need a man, God had blessed me with the resources to provide for me and my children.

I felt stupid, ashamed, and disgusted with myself, for digging this ditch and falling in it. This man dated women during the entire marriage, which lasted until I left in 2014. Yes, I stayed on this merry-go-round for almost thirteen years. I became desensitized to everything going on around me. I managed to leave him once in 2006 and for some reason I told him where I was living.

He came over to visit and my neighbor which was a male was outside washing his truck. My husband pulled up, got out of his truck, greeted me and followed me into my apartment as if everything was okay. Once he got me alone inside, he started accusing me of talking to my neighbor as if we had something going on.

All of a sudden, he started hitting me with his fist and pushing me around. Somehow, I slipped and fell on the floor. Big mistake! I remember it like it was yesterday. He took his foot and started stomping me in the floor like I was a piece of trash. He had slapped and pushed me around but this time he put his foot on me. When we were together, I would rub his feet when he got off work.

After he stomped me, I said to myself I would never put my hands on his feet again. Anger was building up inside of me. I didn't have tears of JOY. My tears had turned into a great deal of bitterness and I wanted revenge. I wanted him to feel the hurt and pain that my helpless body was feeling. The crazy thing is, I allowed him to come back. My emotions were all over the place. I didn't know if I loved him, despised him, or if I just couldn't simply let go.

The enemy allowed him to do everything in his power to tear me down. I don't believe he even remembered half the things he said or did. He would tell me that I wasn't his type and he didn't see how he ever married me. He would tell me he was going to a friend's house, when he was actually going to the lady's house who he worked with.

One day he left her phone number on the table and I looked up the address and went over there. I saw his car parked right next to hers and my heart started pounding. I knocked on the door and he answered. He said he was over his partners house and I corrected him and called him a liar. Of course, he got very upset and defensive. He cursed me out and closed the door in my face. He left me standing there like I was nothing to him.

I couldn't really clown like I wanted to because I had no business being there in the first place. After the fact I thought to myself, what if she had a gun. I had to check myself on that incident. I felt FOOLISH and ASHAMED. I couldn't believe what was happening. I was perplexed to the fifth power. When he got home, I asked him to leave but he wouldn't.

After that it had been occasions where I would see them riding together and she was always smiling. Yes, I could have followed them, but I chose not to. I would hear my mother say, "Every dog has a day and a good dog has two days!" I must admit he was a very handsome man and after getting beat down so much I never felt like I was pretty or sexy enough for him.

I had done it again! I made the mistake of misjudging another man. I was on the edge and all I saw was death. My life had been very hard up to this point and I just wanted the pain to be over. No one should have to endure this type of suffering. I was worthy of love and I knew it, but I was picking the wrong people to receive it from. I was too impatient to wait on God. I was giving God my lip service and my actions in church, but I wasn't allowing Him to fully govern my heart. I wasn't guarding my heart as the word tells us to do. I was leaving it open and those fiery darts from the enemy were coming from near and far.

These men expected love from me, but I guess I wasn't supposed to expect it back in return. Again, I found myself contemplating suicide. I wrestled with death over and over again in my mind. There was no logical reason that one person had to endure so much pain and trauma. This couldn't be the reason and purpose for my life, so maybe I would be better off dead. If I wasn't alive, then I couldn't be abused anymore. I wouldn't continue making emotional mistakes. I needed to rest, and God said to come unto Him if I was burdened and heavy. I was about to create my own death date, because a sister was tired. I was empty and drained. I was holding on by a thread.

By 2009 our relationship was on and off. Our lease was up so we decided to go our separate ways. I knew he was going to move in with the woman that he just couldn't and wouldn't stay away from. I moved with my best friend, but eventually I started missing him. I thought to myself, "What could I possibly be missing?" Did I become immune to being mistreated or was I just out of my mind? It was either, we really did have some good times together. I have always been a comedian by nature, so he laughed at me all the time. There were times when we actually enjoyed each other's company.

A couple of months had gone by and the Lord spoke to me and told me to receive him back in love or let him stay out there with the wolves. I was like, "What?" Yes, I did miss him, but I really wasn't trying to get back with him. No matter how hard I tried to ignore the voice of God, I couldn't rest. I told him what the Lord spoke to me. He wasn't trying to hear that. He was enjoying his life, so I thought.

Days passed and he finally decided he wanted to get back together. So, I got an apartment and it was on again. I really thought everything was going to be peaches and cream, boy was I wrong. He was just as confused as I was, because he couldn't stay away from the woman he was dating.

At that time, I was working twelve hour shifts, so when I came home, he was leaving. One day I confronted him and he said, "I never told you I was going to stop seeing her." I was crushed, but what could I do. We started going to church together and he was very active for a short period of time, but those demons had a strong hold on him, so he moved back in with her.

I didn't blame God. I blamed myself. I asked myself how I could be so stupid. The Holy Spirit spoke to me and said, "Obedience is better than sacrifice." People will tell you this, that, and the other; but when God has you spinning on the potter's wheel, you must make His voice the only voice you harken to. Nevertheless, our relationship still wasn't over, because nothing is over until God say it's over.

It is sad to say, but this man literally cheated the entire relationship. I took a trip to Chicago and he had no clue when I was returning home. I came home early to find an empty house. I didn't call to let him know that I was home, because I wanted to see just how long he was going to be gone with his other woman.

He was gone the entire weekend. I tried calling and he never answered. I could have been hurt, in the hospital, or just needed my husband, but he didn't answer. This is when I decided to stop trying to fight the battle on my own. Yes, I started the war, but I needed help ending it. I went into prayer and prayed the whole night. I told God I wasn't going to let go until He blessed me.

I told God that if I had to remain in this relationship, to please take me, because this man was never satisfied with nothing I attempted to do. After much toiling and pressing I heard the Lord say, He was going to preserve me, give me restored youth, sustain me, and release me from the marriage. I fell asleep and had four very detailed dreams. God was confirming His spoken word through the dreams.

When he finally decided to walk through the door, I begged him not to cheat anymore, but my pleas went unanswered. Around this time, my sister died, and she came to me in a dream and told me to go and get our father. I wasn't sure what I was supposed to do or why, but I followed my sister's instructions against the will of my husband. I went to get my father and moved him in with us. It wasn't five days later that he passed away. I guess the Lord didn't want him to die alone without family.

Here it was, I was already emotionally dead and had to deal with the death of my father and a lying, cheating husband. After everything settled, I went to Chicago again and did the same thing as last time. I didn't tell him when I was returning and arrived home to find him gone. When he came home, I asked him one simple question, "Why do you come home?" I mean if he was so happy being with her, why not stay there?

Why not pack your bags and move in with her? It wasn't making any sense. Apparently, she wanted him, but not enough to keep him.

The devil was on a rampage, doing what he does best. He was working overtime to destroy me and my self-esteem. We sat down to talk, but then he silently got up, walked away and came back with a gun. I was sitting there with a robe on, unsure of his motives and intent for going to get the gun. He didn't actually pull the gun on me, but the fact that he had it made me very nervous.

All I could see was my little short legs running for the door. I sat there contemplating my next move, when I started counting in my mind, "one, two, three" and without hesitating I got up and ran down the stairs and out the door. I stood there and watched as he started putting my things out on the patio.

I didn't really care at this point. I was more concerned about the fact that the gun could have gone off. Then it dawned on me that I didn't have any clothes on, so I went back inside and picked up the phone to call the police. He started wrestling me for the phone and as we were tussling for the phone I got hit in the eye. I couldn't see anything. The pain was extremely excruciating, and I couldn't drive myself to the hospital, so I called my daughter and she came and took me to the hospital. It was so bad I had to have my eye stitched up and the doctor had to remove chips of phone pieces from my face.

That was the final straw. I could have lost my eye, behind his nonsense. He was the one cheating and being unfaithful, yet I was enduring pain and abuse. As much as I didn't want to, I left and went to live with my daughter. I was basically homeless. I found myself sleeping in my car, when I couldn't afford a hotel. My mother told me I couldn't stay with her. I found myself staying in hotel and begging for work just to have a place to lay my head.

This is what my life had come to. After all the hard work of pulling myself up after the first abusive marriage and all the other crap I endured, my life had come to almost nothing. All behind a man and his foolishness. All because I didn't understand my value and my self-worth. I lost everything and I couldn't get a return on my investment, because I had sowed into stony ground. Every man I invested in, did nothing but take and was never able to give what I truly needed – love. This was the most heartbreaking part of all. All I wanted was to be loved. I simply wanted to be seen, but no matter what I felt invisible. Rejection had reared its head so many times in my life that I finally hit rock bottom.

The good thing about hitting rock bottom is that you cant go any lower, the only direction from that dark place is up. I knew that I needed to surrender my will to Gods will and to learn how to patiently wait on Him.

I was praying and trusting that God would make a way out of no way. Proverbs 3:5-6 says, "Trust in the Lord with all thine heart, and LEAN not to your own understanding." As hard as it was, I was trying not to rely on Stephanie's stinking thinking and trying to cast my cares on God, and boy I had so many cares it was unreal. I had to rely on that mustard seed faith, because that was all I had at that time.

When I finally arrived at the point of total faith, God opened an unexpected door. I became friends with this guy who owned some properties. We were talking and I told him about my situation. He listened with great compassion and God moved on his heart to help me. He gave me the keys to one of his condos and I lived there in 2015 and 2017 while in Memphis. This was a somewhat peaceful time for me, because I had to do some work. I had to do some soul searching. I am grateful that God looked past my faults and supplied my need.

When I experienced the death of my mother in 2016, I contacted my estranged husband. I don't know why; I just felt the need to reach out to him. I was feeling vulnerable and alone. Even though we weren't together physically, that soul tie was still very much real in my life. We met up and spent some time together. I realized that despite all the foolishness I did love him or so I thought. Being that I was in a vulnerable state of mind, we slept together. There was a part of me that felt like he may have changed. Part of me wanted him back, because I was lonely and feeling empty.

Once we finished our sexual encounter, the weirdest thing happened. I sat up to get out of the bed and it felt like a weight was lifted or something fell off. I felt lighter and at that moment I remembered what God said. He said he was releasing me from the marriage and that night I was released. We were divorced in 2017 and from that point I started a journey towards healing and restoration. I found myself reflecting on the word of God. That is when it dawned on me that I hadn't been consumed in my mess. God could have allowed me to die in my mess. Did you know that almost 30,000 plus deaths are reported due to domestic violence on a yearly basis? I could have been apart of that number, BUT GOD!

I came to realize that while I kept trying to gratify my flesh, God was trying to mature me in the spirit. This was the farthest thing from my mind, because I just wanted the pain to go away. I didn't realize that I was increasing the pain and intensifying my fears. The years of damage I had done to my mental psyche was unreal. Let's not mention the fact that I had three children and a grandbaby looking at me, depending on me and needing me to be a better example.

It was nothing but the grace of God that I didn't take my own life. It was the favor of God that I wasn't killed. It was the favor of God that helped me when I didn't know how I was going to make it with four mouths to feed and clothe. It wasn't easy, but the power of God prevailed in my life.

Yes, I made some bad choices in men, but to be honest I was working with what I had to work with. You see, many times we don't look at the overall picture. We focus on the negative, which never allows us to see the lessons we were being taught. Life is all about lessons.

This world we live in is a giant textbook and we must be open to the idea that God is speaking all around us.

I was so focused on the bad things, that I missed that part where God was causing ALL things to work out for my good.

Chapter Five

God Had a Purpose, Yet All I Saw Was Pain

Resist him, standing firm in your faith, knowing that the same kinds of suffering are being experienced by your brotherhood throughout the world. **And after you have suffered a little while, the God of all grace, who has called you to his eternal glory in Christ, will himself restore, confirm, strengthen, and establish you.** *1 Peter 5:9-10*

As long as I have lived in the earth, I haven't met a person yet who loves to suffer. There might be some people who can tolerate certain physical pains, but pain is altogether different when its emotional, mental or spiritual. As far back as I can remember I have experienced some very dark days. As a child our greatest concern is being loved, being able to play, and having something to eat.

In my household we played, we had something to eat, but we were lacking in the love department. I won't dare say that my mother didn't love us, but I will say she didn't know how to express it. Was it strictly because of what she endured? Did being a sex slave at such an early age, strip her of her ability to express love?

Did she know that one day she would have children and that they would desire the very things she desired, but didn't receive? These are questions that any normal person would ask. I often questioned God about my life. Wondering why I couldn't be born to another family that didn't have to struggle. Why couldn't I have a family that was supportive and positive?

Why did her pain, have to become my scars? Why couldn't she work on herself before I was born? I tried to be different. I always said I wouldn't make the same mistakes and yet and still, her pain became my scars. Her truth became my truth. Her lies became my lies. Her regrets became my regrets. Her bitterness became my bitterness. Her struggles became my struggles. Her fears became my fears. The things she cried about in secret, I'm almost certain I did the same. There was no escaping the invisible chains that held her bound and captive, even up to the very moment of taking her last breath. The very chains that enslaved the seeds that came from her own womb. We wanted to be free, but God had the master key.

At the time I didn't understand that God had already mapped out my days. It never occurred to me that God was going to use my pain and suffering for His glory. The enemy tried to convince me that I was worthless, and that God didn't love me, but He was with me all the time. God possessed the keys to unlock my destiny. I was so busy fighting trying to yank the chains and break them off myself and it wasn't going to work.

There are no words to describe the pain I felt when I was being touched by people I didn't know or beat by men I trusted. How do I express the feeling that is felt in the pit of your gut, when you are called everything but the name your mother gave you? I can't fathom the thoughts my kids had toward me because of the choices I made, and they had to be included.

There are no words that I could use to paint a pretty picture, because there was nothing pretty about my life. The canvas of my life looked like God just threw a multiplicity of paints on it and said figure out what the drawing entails. He knew what was going on, but I didn't have a clue. To be honest that is pretty much how it is for everyone. We grow up making all these elaborate plans and bam Gods plans kick in and our plans are tossed aside.

I'm sure you've heard the cliché, "If you want to make God laugh; tell Him your plans." I guess that would be pretty funny, trying to tell the Creator and the Sustainer of the universe, how you are going to live the life He provided for His glory. I've come to realize that life is beautiful, but its also confusing.

Job said it best, when he said, "A man born of a woman is of few days and is FULL of trouble." He is a true witness to this fact. I went through some things over the course of my life, but to have the unthinkable happen within the course of a day is something I hope to never experience. My point is this - in our flesh we are racing against time, but when we live according to the spirit, we know that we inherit eternal life.

There are many areas of our lives that we attempt to leave God out of, but to be honest that is absolutely impossible. We couldn't leave God out if we wanted to, because He is the only reason that we live, move and have our being. I had to learn what this meant for my life. I was so busy making unhealthy decisions based on what my mother and father didn't do. I was allowing the course of my life to be altered and riddling my life with pain because I was searching for love in all the wrong places. I had access to the greatest love of all and that was the love of Christ, but I kept purposely forfeiting it for a mediocre man who was insecure and childish.

The greatest lesson I've learned about life is that we have been given the freewill to make choices. I can point my little index finger at those in my circle if I want to, but at the end of the day, God is going to hold me accountable for my actions. This is the hardest test to pass because many times we fail to realize that we are being tested based on our level of spiritual maturity.

We try to live this life based off choices and decisions in the natural, but that only gets us so far in life. If we are unwilling to consult God and to seek answers from the B.I.B.L.E. (basic instructions before leaving earth) then we will never fulfill the purpose, we were created for. My mother took us to church, but in some instances, she failed to take us to God. I had to learn this one for myself and it came through many trials and hardships.

There are many people today, both men and woman who are stuck because of the pain inflicted on them by a parent(s). I was stuck because I didn't understand. I was leaning to my own understanding and basically making a bunch of assumptions. I allowed the enemy to fill my mind with off the wall thoughts that made me feel rejected instead of loved. He was cunning and swift enough to send those wolves in sheep's clothing just when I was feeling the most vulnerable.

At this point I can't go back into my mother's womb to redo my life all over again, but I can start from here. I can take the time to sit back and fully evaluate the course of my life and ask God to show me where I got off track. I can finally take my focus off the pain that ailed me for so long and put my focus on the assignments that God has set forth in my life.

I spent a lot of time trying to please everyone else and Stephanie was suffering. There were very few that were concerned about my level of suffering and even when I didn't include God, He was involved anyway. I love the promises in, 1st Peter 5:10 which says, **"And after you have suffered a little while, the God of all grace, who has called you to his eternal glory in Christ, will himself restore, confirm, strengthen, and establish you."** Did you catch that? It said after you have suffered a little while!

That mean trouble don't last always. Now let me be clear, it can last as short or as long as you want it to. We determine how long we have to stay in time out with God. The scripture calls Him the "God of ALL GRACE!" This mighty and powerful God who has CALLED us to His eternal glory in Christ will HIMSELF:

- Restore – bring back or reinstate
- Confirm – establish the truth or correctness of
- Strengthen – make or become stronger
- Establish – set up on a firm or permanent basis

I don't know about you, but that sounds like good news to me. During the course of my life I lost some things and the enemy stole some things that didn't belong to him and today I decree and declare **restoration**. I thank God that He is **confirming** His promises and that despite my efforts to fall short of His glory from time to time, that He will and is always **strengthening** me. Then most importantly I am grateful that God has **established** His covenant with me through Christ Jesus and I can now live as the righteousness of Christ and no longer in condemnation.

Day by day, God is revealing His purpose for my pain! It would be nice if He revealed it all at one time, but then I'm sure if He did, I would probably mess something up. Not intentionally, but I understand the limitations of my flesh on today and that in my flesh dwells no good thing, which is why I do my best to live according to the spirit. When you start to lose people, who are near and dear to your heart, it stops you in your tracks and causes you to slow down and see the blessings of life from a different set of lenses.

I'm not sure where you are in your life on today. You could be just like me and have endured some traumatic hardships or you could have had a simple life; no matter which one it was, understanding purpose can be hard either way. So, I would admonish you today, to take a long hard look at yourself and ask God to reveal your purpose to you.

There is no need to struggle when He instructed us to, "Call unto Him and He would teach us great and mighty things." Don't miss out or forfeit your blessings, when the One who blesses is ready, willing, and able to answer you and supply your every need according to His riches and glory through Christ Jesus."

But, let me clarify one thing for you, this doesn't mean that the enemy is not going to try you in the area of your faith. When I arrived at the place of trusting God and leaning on him, I had to finally dissect the scripture that says, "No weapon formed against me shall prosper." You see any times we ask God questions, like, "Why me?" or "What did I do wrong?" and many times you have done anything wrong. The enemy's job is to kill, steal and destroy.

As long as we have breath in our bodies he is coming after us with a vengeance, especially if we are sold out to God. There are no ifs, ands or but's about that! He has been after Gods people since the beginning of time and he is not stopping until God stops him at the final day of judgement. In the meantime, between time we have a responsibility to stay alert and aware of satan's devices.

I had to learn this the hard way. After losing my mother, life for me took on a whole different path. I started to reflect on my mother's life, and it gave me a greater awareness of the things I needed to change within myself. I didn't want to die alone and full of regret. I didn't want to live my life battling sickness and disease in the flesh, because of soul wounds and broken heartedness that was hindering my spirit. I wanted to be free and that started with me.

When I started my journey towards a new life, things started looking up for me. I was finding my place in life and when I looked in the mirror, I no longer saw a victim, but a victor. I was gaining strength and momentum but let me testify that the enemy got a whiff of my new God confidence and decided he would come after in a different way. Its one thing to come after me, but its another thing to go after a mother's children.

Yes, the enemy tried to bring me down by attacking my son. He found himself living his life in the streets, chasing after the same thing I was, modeling the same lifestyle of a father he never met. As a mother I tried my best to give my children, the things I didn't receive, but in some areas, I still didn't give them all of me. I found myself experiencing blessings, while feeling cursed all at the same time. There is nothing like a mother's love for her child and in 2019 that love was truly put to the test......

Author Bio

Stephanie Jefferson Martin

is an overcomer. She is a conqueror. She is a fighter. Stephanie is a native of Tennessee, where she grew up on the north side of Memphis. She attended Hollywood Elementary, Kingsbury Junior High and graduated from Westside High School as an Honors Student. Stephanie later attended The University of Memphis and majored in writing. In telling her story she is now advocating for women to stand in their truth and to know who God has called them to be. She is a strong woman of faith, intercessor, and minister. She has three children and married Roy Anthony Martin, Sr. in 2019.

Author Contact Info

Website: www.silentabusebook.com

Email: silentabusebook@gmail.com